The Inca Empire for Kids

A Captivating Guide to the Incas and
Their Civilization, from Early Beginnings
to the Spanish Conquest

Table of Contents

INTRODUCTION

Did you know the Incas were the largest civilization in the Americas before colonization began? They conquered almost the entire Pacific coast of South America, but they were more than just warriors.

In this book, you will learn how the Incas got started, who the most powerful Inca rulers were, and even how the Spanish conquistadors eventually conquered this powerful empire. You'll also learn how the Incas did it all without things like writing or the wheel. Can you imagine building a civilization without writing or the wheel? The Incas certainly could!

This book offers you an in-depth look at the Incas. Both parents and children will enjoy learning about the Inca Empire in this fun, up-to-date history of the Inca people. To meet them, get ready to jump into your time machine and enter a world that was very different than the one we live in today!

Chapter 1: The People before the Incas

The Inca civilization owed a lot to the civilizations that came before them. Peru had many different tribes and civilizations throughout history. They lived all over the west coast of South America before the **Inca Empire** came to power.

The first civilization in Peru that historians know about is the **Norte Chico Civilization**. The Norte Chico Civilization lasted from about 3000 BCE to 1800 BCE. The Norte Chico Civilization is also sometimes called the **Caral Civilization** because **Caral** was the capital city. It is located in north-central Peru, and you can still visit the ruins of the city today. In fact, Caral was the first city ever built in the Americas, which includes both North America and South America. Also, the Norte Chico Civilization was one of only six civilizations to develop separately from any other civilization. They built around 30 cities and created their culture in Peru without help from anyone else. Can you imagine building a city without knowing what one looks like? These first people of Peru certainly could!

The people of the Norte Chico Civilization made flutes and cornets out of animal bones, so they probably enjoyed making music. They also invented a way of counting to keep records called a **quipu**. A quipu is knotted pieces of fabric or cords used to help people keep count of things. That might not sound like a big deal now because we have paper and calculators, but to the ancient people, the quipu was an important invention. It was one of the first ways people communicated without talking face to face.

An example of a quipu Source: Pi3.124; Wikimedia Commons

The people of the Norte Chico Civilization were clearly inventive, but they did not make pottery of any kind. In fact, they created barely any art. Can you imagine living in a world without any art? The only thing the people of the Norte Chico Civilization made that could be art was their architecture. They built pyramids and plazas. The design of their cities was so well-thought-out that other civilizations built their cities like the Norte Chico Civilization.

After the Norte Chico Civilization, the next really important civilizations in Peru were the **Moche Civilization** and the **Nazca Civilization**. These two civilizations existed at the same time, from 100 CE to 800 CE, but they were in different areas of Peru.

The Moche people lived in northern Peru near the coast. Their capital city is called **Moche City** today. They are famous for their farming and **irrigation systems**, which allowed them to water all of their crops. The Moche Civilization is also famous for its art. They made pottery that was often designed to look like people or animals. The pottery was elaborate and startlingly life-like.

Moche Pottery Source: https://flic.kr/p/WGcPNJ

The Moche people also built impressive temples, which are called **huacas**. They are made out of **adobe bricks**. Their two most famous temples are called the **Pyramid of the Moon** and the **Pyramid of the Sun**. The Pyramid of the Sun was made with 130 million adobe bricks! Can you imagine how long it would take to make that many bricks by hand?

The Moche people also made beautiful jewelry, such as earrings and necklaces.

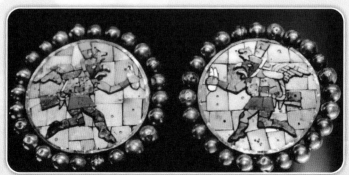

Pair of ear ornaments from Peru (Moche) ca. 200-600 CE
Source: https://flic.kr/p/ZE2YwT

The Nazca Civilization was different from the Moche Civilization. The Nazca people lived on the southern coast of Peru. They fished a lot, but they also farmed crops like **maize** (which is a type of corn), squash, and sweet potatoes. There is a lot of desert land in southern Peru, so the Nazca people built **aqueducts** to move water around. These aqueducts were so well built that they still work today!

The Nazca were brilliant artists and worked with textiles and pottery, but they are the most famous for the **Nazca Lines**. The Nazca Lines are huge drawings in the Nazca Desert around the cities of Palpa and Nazca. There are drawings of birds, monkeys, llamas, dogs, and spiders. The drawings were carved into the ground by removing dark stones to expose the lighter sand beneath.

Nazca Lines—the Spider Source: https://flic.kr/p/r5uPTT

The Nazca Lines are huge. Some of them are over 600 feet long! They are so big that you can't really see them on the ground. Instead, you have to fly over the Nazca Desert to really see these drawings. Historians don't know yet how the Nazca people were able to draw the Nazca Lines. They also don't know why the Nazca people even drew them. This is one of the mysteries that historians are still trying to solve. For now, we can still be amazed every time we see the Nazca Lines.

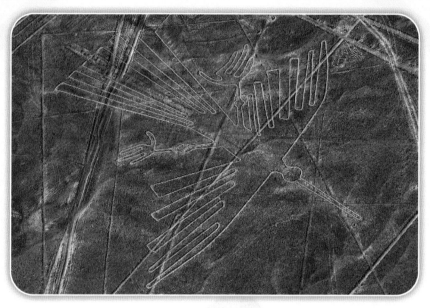

Nazca Lines—the Condor
Source: https://commons.wikimedia.org/wiki/File:The_Condor_(226411781).jpeg#/media/File:The_Condor_(226411781).jpeg

The next important civilization in Peru was the **Tiahuanaco Civilization** (tee-uh-wuh-naa-kow). This civilization is also called **Tiwanaku**, and it lasted from about 300 CE to 1000 CE. They lived in southern Peru and in northern Chile. They built large cities out of stone. The biggest city of the Tiahuanaco Civilization has several impressive buildings, including one called the **Kalasasaya**. The Kalasasaya is a rectangular building that has the **Gateway of the Sun** in it. The Gateway of the Sun has carvings of a **doorway god** and seems to have been very important to the Tiwanaku people. A doorway god is a deity in charge of guarding doors against evil spirits. They are usually painted or carved onto doors to protect the building.

The Tiahuanaco Civilization had a lot in common with the **Huari Civilization** (wah-ree). The Huari Civilization lasted from 600 CE to 900 CE, which is during the same time as the Tiahuanaco Civilization. These two groups lived right next to each other, so it makes sense that they would share a lot of their culture with each other.

Map of the Huari and Tiahuanaco

The Huari people were warlike, and they conquered a lot of the coastline of Peru. However, they also shared some cultural ideas with the Tiahuanaco people. The Huari decorated their pottery with the same doorway god that the Tiahuanaco people used. Their buildings and temples are also similar to the buildings of the Tiwanaku people.

Another important similarity was their inventive forms of farming. The Huari people used **terraced farming** in the mountains. They would carve out flat sections into the mountainside and stack these sections like big stairs. This allowed them to grow more food than the mountain could produce on its own. The Tiahuanaco used a similar form of farming called a **raised field system**. They separated all of their farming fields with canals. The water in the canals absorbed the heat from the sun and kept the crops from freezing during the night.

The last complex civilization in Peru before the Incas arrived was the **Chimú Civilization**. They conquered much of Peru's coastline, and their capital city was **Chan Chan**. Chan Chan is the largest adobe city in the Americas, and the city must have housed thousands of people! Can you imagine living with thousands of people in an adobe city?

The Chimú people had to make sure they had plenty of water. The city had ten different citadels, each with its own temples and water reservoirs. The walls of Chan Chan are covered with beautiful carvings.

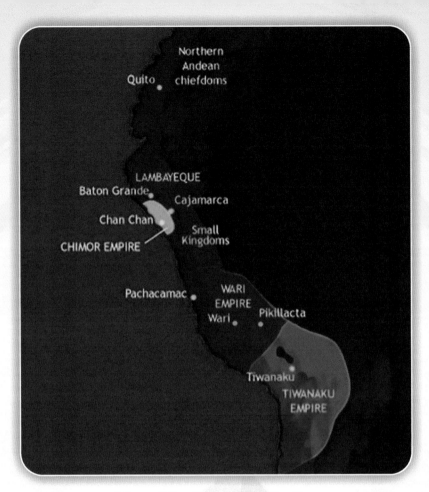

Map of the Chimú Civilization

The Chimú culture was very orderly. There were no questions about your social position in the city. They focused on agriculture, metalwork, and pottery. When the Inca conquered the Chimú Civilization around 1470 CE, they took much of the Chimú culture for themselves.

Chapter 1 Challenge: Vocabulary Matching

Can you match the vocabulary word with its description?

1. Chimú Civilization

    a. The capital city of the Norte Chico Civilization and the first city in the Americas

2. Nazca Civilization

    b. This civilization was also called Tiwanaku. It lasted from 300 CE to 1000 CE. The last important civilization in Peru before the Incas

3. Tiahuanaco Civilization

    c. The capital of this civilization was Moche City, and they made pottery shaped like animals and people.

4. Huari Civilization

    d. The civilization in southern Peru from 100 CE to 800 CE

5. Moche Civilization

    e. Animal shaped carvings in the ground of the Nazca desert

6. Norte Chico Civilization

    f. The militaristic civilization next door to Tiahuanaco who practiced terrace farming

7. Nazca Lines

    g. The first civilization in Peru

8. Caral

Chapter 2: The First Incas

The **Incas** did not start as the powerful civilization we remember them as. Just like every other civilization, the Incas were small and unknown when they started building their empire. Of course, they would grow to be one of the most powerful empires in the Americas. They would rule almost the whole coast of the **Pacific Ocean** and throughout the **Andes Mountains**. They did it all without some of the things that historians normally say a civilization needs. The Incas did not have wheels or cast iron. Can you imagine a world without wheels? Getting anywhere would be a challenge!

The Incas also did not have a system of writing. Everything we know about the Incas was written down by the **Spanish conquistadors**, who heard the Inca history as a verbal story. We have to be careful with the

Map of the Inca territory over the centuries

stories told by the Spanish conquistadors because they wanted to make their conquests seem like a good thing. They might not have retold the Inca stories accurately, but these stories are a great place to start learning about the Incas. Historians also rely on archaeology to learn more about the Incas, and they are learning more all the time.

The Incas have two different stories about how they began. The first story is their origin myth. According to the myth, the sun god **Inti** looked down one day and saw how sad the early people of the world were. They didn't have clothes, houses, or cities. It was a hard time for humankind. Inti wanted to help the people, so he sent one of his sons and one of his daughters to Earth to teach the people how to be better.

His son's name was **Manco Cápac**, and his daughter's name was **Mama Ocllo**. They were also married. Marrying your sibling is weird today, but the Incas didn't think it was weird. In fact, they thought it was normal for kings to marry their sisters! The legend says that they appeared from a cave in **Paccari Tampu**, which was the village the first Incas lived in. They taught the people how to farm and how to build houses. They also took the people away from Paccari Tampu in search of a better place to build a city. Inti had told his children to build their city in a spot where they could drive a golden stake into the ground with only one hit. They eventually found a place in modern-day Peru, and they named their new city **Cuzco**.

Historians don't think this myth is completely accurate, but they have noticed some similarities between the myth and the more historically accurate explanation. The Incas did live in a small village in the Andes Mountains until about the 12th century. Then, around 1200 CE, Manco Cápac led the Inca people about 15 miles north. There, they built, which remained the Cuzco capital of the Incas throughout their empire.

You probably noticed there are some similarities between these two stories. Manco Cápac is the first leader of the Incas that we know about, but historians don't think he was the son of Inti. The Incas used the myth of Inti to justify their conquests. They believed that the sun god wanted them to grow and thrive. This meant conquering their neighbors, who they thought were not blessed by Inti.

Manco Cápac
Source: https://commons.wikimedia.org/wiki/
File:Ayarmanco1.JPG#/media/File:Ayarmanco1.JPG

The Incas began building Cuzco, but for several hundred years, they were very similar to the other tribes that lived near them. Manco Cápac is remembered for starting the Inca dynasty and for moving the people to their new capital. His son was **Sinchi Roca**, who continued to build Cuzco and protect it from other tribes living near the Incas.

Sinchi Roca

The Incas didn't really make history until their fourth ruler took the throne. In the 1300s, **Mayta Cápac** became the fourth ruler of the Inca people. Mayta Cápac is remembered as a great warrior. Many of the Inca kings were warrior kings, but Mayta Cápac was the first Inca ruler to use his warrior skills to start expanding the Kingdom of Cuzco. Instead of focusing on protecting Cuzco, Mayta Cápac began to take his army out to conquer nearby villages in the valley. They would attack these villages and **loot** them, which means they stole anything they wanted. Some historians think the Incas might have also required the conquered villages to pay tribute, which is like a tax.

Mayta Cápac never left the valley that Cuzco was in. He was satisfied with conquering all the villages there first. The ruler who came after him was named **Cápac Yupanqui**, and he started taking the Inca conquests outside Cuzco Valley. Those expeditions were small, but they still expanded the Kingdom of Cuzco. Instead of trying to conquer the whole Pacific coast at once, the Incas took their conquests slowly. They made sure they wouldn't lose their empire too soon by conquering too much land at once.

These small conquests were an essential part of the Inca ruling culture until the eighth ruler came to power in the early 1400s. His name was **Viracocha Inca**, and he is the person who really made the Incas a conquering civilization. Viracocha Inca worked with his uncles and created the first serious Inca army. With his new army, Viracocha Inca marched out of Cuzco Valley and challenged the **Ayarmaca** people. They lived in the **Urubamba Valley**, which was close by.

After a big fight, the Incas defeated the Ayarmaca people and took over the Urubamba Valley. The Incas renamed the valley the **Sacred Valley of the Incas**. Viracocha Inca realized that the Incas needed a way to keep peace and defend their new lands, especially as the Incas continued to expand and conquer other tribes around them. He knew that some of the people he conquered might be angry with the Incas. Can you imagine how you would feel if the Incas had just conquered your city? It might be a little scary, or you might feel upset that strangers just took over your home.

Viracocha Inca wanted to prevent any of the people he conquered from fighting back after he was gone. So, he started the Inca tradition of building **garrisons** in all of the lands the Incas conquered. A garrison is a military base that usually has soldiers in it. They defend the town they're in and keep the people from revolting.

The Incas would continue to build garrisons as they expanded. Inca rulers constantly looked for more wealth, power, and land. Once the Incas figured out how to conquer nearby villages, they used that to grow their empire into the powerful civilization we remember today.

Can you put the names of these rulers in chronological order?

!   Manco Cápac

!   Cápac Yupanqui

!   Sinchi Roca

!   Viracocha Inca

!   Mayta Cápac

Chapter 3: The Inca Empire

Although the Incas had existed long before their empire began, **Pachacuti Inca Yupanqui** is credited with founding the **Inca Empire** in 1438 CE. At the height of its power, the Inca Empire was huge. It ran along the Pacific coast of South America, stretching out about 3,400 miles (5,500 kilometers). The Incas spread out across modern-day countries like Peru, Ecuador, Colombia, Chile, Argentina, and Bolivia. The city farthest to the north was called **Quito**, and the city farthest to the south was called **Santiago**.

The Inca Empire was the largest empire in the Americas. It was also one of the largest empires in the world in the 1400s! Historians think there were about 10 million people who lived in the Inca Empire at the height of

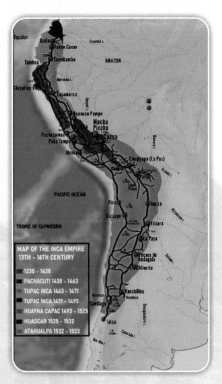

Map illustrating the expansion of the Inca Empire
from its origins in the 13th century until the 16th century

its power. The Incas had to keep the peace and prevent crimes while also holding onto all the power and lands that they had conquered. Can you imagine trying to do all that while organizing 10 million people?

To keep everything organized, the Incas had to make a structured government. To make things even harder, the Incas never invented a written language. They had to rely on **oral messages**. If you have ever played the Telephone Game, you know how challenging it can be to get verbal messages completely right.

The only thing that the Incas used that resembles written communication was called a **quipu**. A quipu was a series of ropes that the Incas used to record information. It mostly recorded numbers, like how many years a king had ruled or how much was gathered in taxes. It wasn't really helpful for recording information that didn't involve numbers, like names or places.

To communicate all of that information, the Incas built an organized road system that ran all over the Inca Empire. If you were to walk every single road in the Inca Empire, you would walk about 14,900 miles. The four main highways ran out from Cuzco, the capital of the Inca Empire. That meant that all roads eventually led to Cuzco.

But the Incas never invented the wheel. This means that they didn't have carts or chariots. If they wanted to go anywhere, they would have to ride an animal or walk. They invented a system of relay runners. These runners were stationed on the roads to take messages and goods anywhere in the empire. It would have been similar to our mail system today. People would give their messages or packages to a runner, and they would take it wherever it needed to go. And they were fast! The runners worked together, so they could move messages and goods about 150 miles in one day. That's really far, especially when running!

The Incas didn't just build impressive roads. They also had to adapt to the different landscapes in their empire. The Inca Empire had all kinds of landscapes, like mountains, deserts, plains, and jungles. They figured out how to build **aqueducts** to move water to dry areas. They also figured out how to **terrace farm**, which is when a farmer makes the sloped sides of mountains look like really big stairs. They would plant different crops on each flat portion, which helped the farmers grow more food. The Incas also built roads and bridges through the tropical jungles to help their runners move quickly without having to climb up and down rivers and small canyons. Despite the many different landscapes in the empire, the Incas managed to build some very impressive cities, roads, and temples.

The man who started the Inca Empire on its path to greatness was **Pachacuti Inca Yupanqui**. He was the ninth ruler, and he ruled the Incas from 1438 CE to 1471 CE. Pachacuti first came to power in 1438 during an invasion of Cuzco by the **Chanca** people. The king of the Incas had fled to a nearby military fort, so Pachacuti took responsibility for defending the city. He drove out the Chancas and became the first emperor of the Incas.

Pachacuti then began to conquer villages outside of Cuzco Valley, something that the rulers before him had never taken seriously. Because of his bold ambitions, Pachacuti is remembered as one of the greatest Inca rulers. He started the rapid growth of the Inca Empire, which would last through most of its existence.

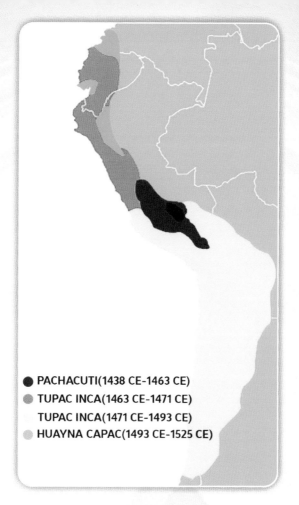

Map of the expansion of the Inca Empire from 1438 CE to 1533 CE

https://commons.wikimedia.org/wiki/File:Inca_Expansion.svg#/media/File:Inca_Expansion.svg

- PACHACUTI(1438 CE-1463 CE)
- TUPAC INCA(1463 CE-1471 CE)
- TUPAC INCA(1471 CE-1493 CE)
- HUAYNA CAPAC(1493 CE-1525 CE)

But Pachacuti isn't only remembered for being a great general. Remember, he became the emperor after a huge attack on Cuzco by the Chanca people. The city needed a lot of repairs. Pachacuti made all of those repairs, but there are stories that he did more than that. According to some of the stories, Pachacuti rebuilt the city to look like a puma. Can you imagine what living in a city shaped like a ferocious cat might be like? The temples were near the head, but the river was near the tail. You would have to walk a long way to get to the river! Only royalty and government officials were allowed to live in the city.

Everyone else had to live in little villages around the city.

Historians don't know if Cuzco was really shaped like a puma. When the Inca Empire fell to the Spanish conquistadors, the Spanish took all of the gold and destroyed the city. They then built another city on top of the ruins of Cuzco. That makes it harder for archaeologists to investigate the city that Pachacuti rebuilt while he was the emperor of the Incas.

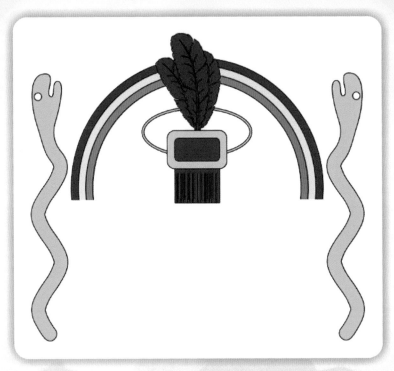

Reconstruction of the banner of Inca emperors. (Source: https://commons.wikimedia.org/wiki/File:Banner_of_the_Inca_Empire.svg# /media/File:Banner_of_the_Inca_Empire.svg

Pachacuti built many different cities and forts all over his empire. The most famous one is called **Machu Picchu**. Pachacuti founded Machu Picchu around 1450 CE. Although it survived the Spanish conquest, historians don't really know what the purpose of this isolated place was. A lot of historians think Machu Picchu was a religious center. It has a lot of temples and roads that lead to nearby towns. You can still visit Machu

Picchu today and see how the Incas built their temples and cities. It's like stepping back in time.

While Pachacuti was conquering land for the Incas and building cities, he also made some changes to the Inca government that would help the empire thrive. He started by allowing anyone who spoke **Quechua**, which was the Inca language, to become a citizen of the Inca Empire. This meant that you had more rights than other people.

One of those rights was being part of the government. Pachacuti restructured the government to make it better for a growing empire. He made a tax system for the people the Incas conquered, which helped the Inca Empire get more wealth and power. Taxes were usually paid in goods or in labor. The Incas stored the goods in storehouses, and they used laborers to build the roads that ran all over the empire.

The last thing that Pachacuti did before he died was conquer the **Chimú Civilization**. This happened at **Chan Chan** around 1470 CE. When Pachacuti died in 1471, everyone mourned him for a whole year. That's a really long time!

Túpac Inca Yupanqui was Pachacuti's son, and he became the next emperor of the Incas. He continued Pachacuti's plan to conquer the lands around the Incas. Túpac Inca Yupanqui was so successful that by the time his reign was over, the Inca Empire had doubled in size. The Inca Empire quickly grew to become one of the greatest civilizations of the Americas because it had strong leaders who wanted to help their people grow.

Chapter 3 Challenge: True or False

Can you identify which statements are true and which statements are false?

1. Pachacuti built Machu Picchu.   _____

2. The Incas had a complex system of writing that
   historians have not learned how to read yet.   _____

3. The Incas only built roads going to major cities in their
   empire.   _____

4. Pachacuti came up with a taxation system that helped
   the Incas grow in power and wealth.   _____

5. The Incas used quipus to record information.   _____

6. Pachacuti helped the Inca Empire double in size by the
   time his reign was over.   _____

7. Historians think Machu Picchu was a big military base.   _____

8. The Incas adapted to all types of landscapes to make
   their empire strong.   _____

Chapter 4: The Kingdom of Cuzco

Cuzco was the capital of the Inca Empire, but it was more than just an important political city. For the Incas, Cuzco was the center of the world. This was both literally and spiritually. All of their roads led to Cuzco because they thought their capital was the most important place on the planet. Cuzco also had some of the most impressive temples, making it the center of Inca religious activity. Can you imagine having that much power in one place?

Before it became the Inca Empire, it was first known as the Kingdom of Cuzco. This chapter is going to focus on the city of Cuzco. We'll talk about how the city became so important and what made it famous.

Just like all the other cities in the world, **Cuzco** (which is also spelled Cusco) was not built in one day. It was built over many years in an ancient valley way up in the Andes Mountains. The city was a little over 11,100 feet above sea level. That's 37 football fields stacked on top of each other!

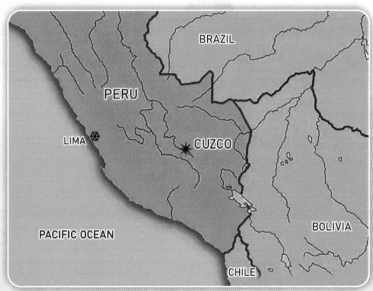

Location of Cuzco on the map

Cuzco also sat in the spot where three rivers met. Those rivers are called the **Huatanay**, **Tullumayo**, and **Chunchul**. Today, the spot is in southern Peru. The Incas thought the spot was really special. That's why they chose to build their capital city there.

Cuzco was settled by the Incas around 1200 CE by the first king of the Incas. His name was **Manco Cápac**. You might remember that he was thought to be the son of **Inti**, the sun god. Inti sent Manco Cápac to help the Incas become big and powerful, and he led the Incas out of their little village and founded Cuzco.

Cuzco didn't begin to really grow until after 1438 CE. The Incas defeated the **Chancas** that year. After that, Emperor **Pachacuti Inca** focused on making Cuzco the best city in the world. To do that, Pachacuti Inca rebuilt the entire city! He moved buildings around, tore up the roads, and even drained the swamps that were nearby. It must have been really chaotic to live in Cuzco while all of that rebuilding was going on. How would you have liked to live in Cuzco during Pachacuti Inca's renovations?

Some historians think that Pachacuti Inca redesigned Cuzco to look like a **puma** or a **jaguar**. The main city was the body of the puma. The head was the temple complexes, and the tail was the imperial palaces. Did you know that there were multiple royal palaces in Cuzco? That's because each emperor built a new palace for himself.

The city had a lot of buildings. Most of them were small and built around open courtyards. There were a few important buildings that were amazing. One of those buildings was **Coricancha**. Coricancha was a huge temple complex. Each of the temples was built in honor of different Inca gods. This was the most sacred place for the Incas, and they thought Coricancha was the center of the world.

According to the stories we have, the **Temple of the Sun** was covered in gold because it was dedicated to Inti, the sun god. All of the walls were lined with gold, and the doors were also covered in gold. If that wasn't enough, there were also a lot of gold statues and other gold objects. Part of the reason there was so much gold at Coricancha was because the Incas thought that gold was actually the sun's sweat. By bringing it back into the Temple of the Sun, they thought they were honoring Inti.

The temple also had a garden. You might think that a god's garden might have beautiful flowers or really good food, but the garden for Inti didn't have any of those things. Instead, it was full of plants and animals that were all made from gold and silver.

Entrance into Coricancha
Source: https://commons.wikimedia.org/wiki
/File:Coricancha_Eingang.jpg#/media/File:Coricancha_Eingang.jpg

Coricancha was a great example of Inca architecture. The Incas had figured out how to build walls by cutting and stacking rocks together so well that they didn't need any mortar to stick the rocks together. That would have taken a lot of planning! The temple complex also had a special underground river, dedicated places for human sacrifice, and a special place for the **mummies** of past emperors. Did you think that the Egyptians were the only civilization to make mummies? They actually weren't! The Incas did as well. They even used the mummies of past emperors during large religious celebrations.

Of course, Coricancha wasn't the only impressive building in Cuzco. The **emperor's palaces** were stunning, and every emperor built his own palace. The Incas believed the spirit of the dead emperor continued to live in his old palace, and they didn't want to intrude on that. Another really important building was **Sacsayhuamán**. This building was on the other side of Cuzco from Coricancha. Historians think that it was a military fortress.

Sacsayhuamán ruin at Cuzco
Source: https://en.wikipedia.org/wiki/Sacsayhuam%C3%A1n#/media/File:
Sacsayhuam%C3%A1n,_Cusco,_Per%C3%BA,_2015-07-31,_DD_28-30_PAN.JPG

The walls of Sacsayhuamán are impressive. The walls were made of huge stones that fit together. Some of the rocks weigh more than 200 tons! Can you imagine trying to move something that weighed about as much as 100 elephants? Historians think that it must have taken more than 20,000 men to build Sacsayhuamán.

Sacsayhuamán ruin at Cuzco Source: https://flic.kr/p/2kUXKWf

Sacsayhuamán also had buildings inside the walls. Some of these buildings might have been temples and houses. There were also roads and **aqueducts** to bring in water. This fortress was ready for the Incas to use whenever they had to defend themselves from enemies.

Sacsayhuamán ruin at Cuzco
Source: https://commons.wikimedia.org/wiki/File:Walls_
at_Sacsayhuaman.jpg#/media/File:Walls_at_Sacsayhuaman.jpg

You can still see the ruins of Sacsayhuamán today, but we can no longer look at most of these impressive Inca buildings anymore. When the **Spanish conquistadors** arrived in the 1500s, they conquered the Incas. When they did, they destroyed Cuzco. They took all of the gold and sent it to Spain. They burned down the buildings and broke down the walls. The Spaniards built a new city on top of where Cuzco had been. All we have left of Cuzco are the few ruins that survived and stories of the Spanish conquistadors who saw Cuzco in all of its golden glory.

Chapter 4 Challenge: Creative Activity

The buildings in Cuzco were reported to be some of the most impressive in the whole Inca Empire, but other than some descriptions, we don't know what they looked like! Drawing things can help us figure that out. Can you draw what the Temple of the Sun might have looked like?

Remember, the Incas covered the walls and doors with gold. Some stories even say that there were emeralds on the walls! The Incas also had golden statues. One of the statues was of Inti when he was a small boy. Another piece of art in the temple was a mask that looked like the sun on the horizon, with beams of light coming off of it.

The Incas also had a garden for the Temple of Sun. It was filled with gold and silver plants and animals. These included things like ears of corn, llamas, guinea pigs, butterflies, monkeys, and even jaguars. Everything in the garden was life-sized, so don't be afraid to draw big! How do you think the Temple of the Sun looked at the height of the Inca Empire?

Chapter 5: The Story of Machu Picchu

Machu Picchu is the most famous part of the Inca Empire. Some people even call it the "Lost City of the Incas." Although it was never lost to the native people in that part of the Andes Mountains, it was lost to the Spanish conquistadors. They never found it! Machu Picchu still exists much as how the Incas left it, so it's one of the best places to explore the culture of the Inca Empire.

Machu Picchu (Source: https://flic.kr/p/GaWFb9)

Machu Picchu was built high up in the **Andes Mountains**. It was about 50 miles northwest of Cuzco, and it is completely surrounded by mountains. There is a river that runs nearby called the **Urubamba River**. Machu Picchu is located in modern-day southern Peru. You can still visit it today! Thousands of tourists make the journey every year to see Machu Picchu.

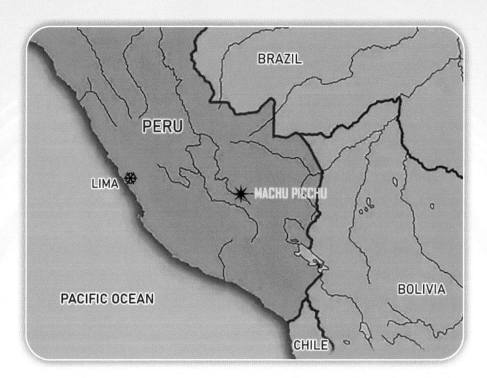

Location of Machu Picchu on the map

Part of the reason that people continue to be fascinated by Machu Picchu is that we don't really know much about it. Remember, the Incas never developed a way to write things down. Without writing things down, it's hard for other people to know what the purpose of everything really is. It would be like trying to go to the grocery store without a list. Have you ever done that with your parents? It's hard to remember everything when you left the list at home!

There are no written stories about Machu Picchu. Archaeologists pieced together all the information we have from the clues that the Incas left behind. The buildings of Machu Picchu were probably built by **Emperor Pachacuti Inca**. He was the first emperor who seriously started expanding the Inca Empire outside Cuzco Valley, so that makes sense.

Historians also think that Machu Picchu was abandoned around 100 years after it was built. Archaeologists have used **radiocarbon dating** to figure out the ages of the buildings and other things in the area. Radiocarbon dating is a special test that archaeologists and scientists can do on old artifacts. As things get older, they lose certain molecules at a predictable rate. Radiocarbon dating measures how much of a particular type of carbon molecule is in each thing. The less carbon there is, the older the thing is. By doing radiocarbon dating on the things at Machu Picchu, archaeologists have found that the site was used from around 1450 to 1532 CE.

Around 1532 CE, historians think that Machu Picchu was abandoned. The Spanish conquistadors never found it, so it wasn't abandoned because the conquistadors were attacking it. Some historians think Machu Picchu was abandoned because of how hard it was to get water. Other historians think that a **smallpox epidemic** made everyone leave. Once everyone left, Machu Picchu was hidden from the world until an American archaeologist named **Hiram Bingham** found the city in 1911. Some of the local people showed him the ruins, and Hiram Bingham was so excited that he shared them with the world.

Ever since that big discovery, historians have been trying to figure out what Machu Picchu was built for. There have been a lot of different ideas. Some people think it used to be a fortress because of its strong walls. Other historians think it was a ceremonial or religious city. There are several stunning temples at Machu Picchu. It's also very close to the mountains, which the Incas thought were sacred. Currently, most historians think Machu Picchu was a royal retreat, like a vacation house for the emperor.

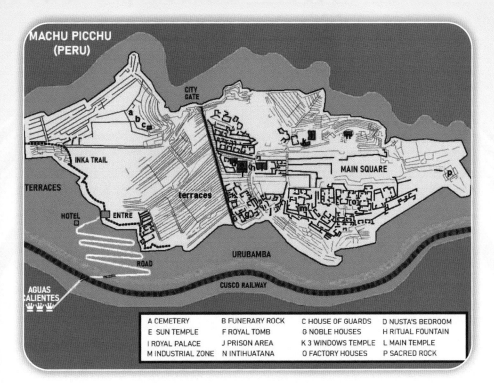

MACHU PICCHU
(PERU)

CITY GATE

INKA TRAIL

TERRACES

terraces

MAIN SQUARE

HOTEL   ENTRE

ROAD

URUBAMBA

AGUAS CALIENTES

CUSCO RAILWAY

A CEMETERY	B FUNERARY ROCK	C HOUSE OF GUARDS	D NUSTA'S BEDROOM
E SUN TEMPLE	F ROYAL TOMB	G NOBLE HOUSES	H RITUAL FOUNTAIN
I ROYAL PALACE	J PRISON AREA	K 3 WINDOWS TEMPLE	L MAIN TEMPLE
M INDUSTRIAL ZONE	N INTIHUATANA	O FACTORY HOUSES	P SACRED ROCK

Map of Machu Picchu

Although historians are still deciding what Machu Picchu was built for, we can admire how good the Incas were at building. Machu Picchu is full of classic Inca architecture. The buildings and steps showcase how the Incas would fit stones together without using mortar. They also used terraces to increase their crops on the sides of the mountains.

Although there are about 150 buildings in Machu Picchu, there are three buildings that are really impressive. The first building is called **Inti Mach'ay**. Inti Mach'ay was more of a cave than a building, but it was the most important structure in Machu Picchu. The windows on Inti Mach'ay are special. Instead of being large and rectangular like our windows are today, the windows on Inti Mach'ay are long and thin, like a tunnel. This means sunlight could only come through the windows on certain days around the winter solstice.

Historians think that Inti Mach'ay was a special building where the royalty would observe the **Royal Feast of the Sun**. This was a special feast that was celebrated around the winter solstice. The building was not used at any other time during the year. However, the Incas built Inti Mach'ay with such care because it was important to their religion.

The second important building at Machu Picchu is the **Sacred Rock**, which is also called the **Temple of the Sun**. The Temple of the Sun in Machu Picchu looked similar to the Temple of the Sun in Cuzco. The Sacred Rock at Machu Picchu has several windows. Historians have found that the windows all seem to be placed in a way that allows them to line up with either the sun or different constellations. The two big windows are shaped like **trapezoids**, which the Incas did in a lot of other buildings too. These two big windows line up with the summer solstice. One of the windows shows the sun rising on the summer solstice, and one of the windows shows the sun setting on the summer solstice. Clearly, the movement of the sun was very important to the Incas!

The third important structure at Machu Picchu is **Intihuatana**. Intihuatana can be translated into English as the "Hitching Post of the Sun." It was a sundial! But Intihuatana was not an ordinary sundial. It was carved out of one piece of rock, and it stands about six feet tall. That's as tall as some grown men! The top of the sundial points almost directly at the sun during the winter solstice. The Incas believed that Intihuatana kept the sun on its path during the whole year. That made Intihuatana one of the most sacred structures in the whole city of Machu Picchu.

The Sacred Valley (Source: https://flic.kr/p/2bu4GJb)

You can visit Machu Picchu today and see these great buildings for yourself. Peru is working hard to preserve and restore the ruins at Machu Picchu. It is one of the UNESCO World Heritage Sites, so as long as we are respectful, we should be able to enjoy Machu Picchu for years to come. Hopefully, by that time, historians will have learned even more about the Inca Empire from the ruins that were left behind.

Machu Picchu is not the only UNESCO World Heritage Site. UNESCO stands for United Nations Educational, Scientific, and Cultural Organization. It is an international group that protects areas, landmarks, and buildings that are really special to humanity as a whole. There are many different areas that have been labeled as World Heritage Sites, which means they are under UNESCO's protection.

Chapter 5 Challenge: True or False

Can you identify which statements are true and which statements are false?

1. Historians think that Machu Picchu was a royal retreat for the emperor. _____

2. Machu Picchu was used by the Incas for 500 years. _____

3. The Temple of the Sun in Machu Picchu has two windows for watching the winter solstice. _____

4. Hiram Bingham found Machu Picchu in 1911 with the help of some of the local people. _____

5. Machu Picchu was built high up in the Andes Mountains. _____

6. The Incas used Inti Mach'ay for eating dinner every day. _____

7. Historians think that Machu Picchu was built by Emperor Pachacuti Inca. _____

8. The Incas abandoned Machu Picchu because the Spanish conquistadors made them leave the city. _____

Chapter 6: The Fall of the Inca Empire

Everything comes to an end. Even powerful empires fall apart and collapse. The Inca Empire was no different. Even though the Inca Empire was full of strong warriors, they encountered several problems all at once. Any one of these problems would have weakened the Incas for a time. Since they happened at the same time, they caused the Inca Empire to collapse.

The first problem the Inca Empire had to deal with was **diseases**. The Spanish were beginning to explore Central and South America. Although they didn't intend to, the Spanish brought all kinds of illnesses with them. These were illnesses like the flu, smallpox, chickenpox, and measles. These were common diseases in Europe, so the Spanish already had **immunization** (protection) against these germs. The people who lived in Central and South America did not. That caused a **pandemic** to sweep through Central and South America.

Historians estimate that 50 to 90 percent of the people living in Central and South America died from the diseases the Spanish accidentally brought over from Europe. Can you imagine what would happen to your city if you suddenly lost half of the people living there? A lot of jobs wouldn't get done because there wouldn't be enough people.

The Incas faced this problem. They suddenly didn't have enough people to grow all the food they needed or enough people to run messages throughout the empire. People were dying from the flu (which is also called **influenza**) and **smallpox**. The nobles also got sick and died from these diseases. That started to create problems about who would be the next emperor because the **line of succession** (who would rule next) was not easy to figure out.

Another problem that the Incas were dealing with was **rebellions**. Now, the Incas often dealt with rebellions. They were constantly expanding their empire, and that meant they were constantly conquering other civilizations. The people the Incas conquered usually weren't happy about that. Every time the Incas conquered more land, they had to also put down rebellions. That allowed them to keep their new land and continue to grow their empire.

In the early 1500s, the Incas were conquering part of modern-day Ecuador. They were also establishing a new city for themselves named **Quito**. The Incas were planning for Quito to become the second capital of the empire, but they were never able to finish that plan.

The third problem that the Incas had to deal with was a civil war that broke out between two royal brothers. In 1527, **Emperor Huayna Capac** died of smallpox. His oldest son, Ninan Cuyochi, also died of smallpox at the same time. This made it very difficult for the Incas to decide who would be the next emperor.

Two of Emperor Huayna Capac's sons wanted to be the emperor. Huáscar thought he should be the next emperor because he was next in line. He was also already in charge of Cuzco, the capital of the Inca Empire. His half-brother Atahualpa thought that he should be the emperor because he was a better warrior. He had also been in charge of conquering Quito for the Inca Empire. Atahualpa wasn't technically in the line of succession, so Huáscar didn't think his half-brother should be emperor. The two brothers weren't able to come to an agreement, and they went to war.

When the war began, Huáscar had most of the people's loyalty. He was based in Cuzco, so most of the Incas believed that Huáscar was the rightful ruler. Atahualpa had the bigger army. Although support is nice during a war, generals also need to have enough soldiers to fight the battles.

The Inca Civil War

Map describing the Inca Civil War

Huáscar tried to end the war quickly by marching on Quito. He thought that if he took Quito, he could stop any support that Atahualpa had. Huáscar fought bravely, but he was not able to take the city. Instead, he was pushed back. Atahualpa's army followed him all the way to Cuzco. Atahualpa's army terrorized tribes along the way who sided with Huáscar. Atahualpa was trying to show that he was more powerful than his brother. It would end up costing Atahualpa dearly in the end.

In 1532, there was a big battle outside of Cuzco between the armies of the two brothers. Huáscar was defeated and taken prisoner. Atahualpa was away in the north when the battle happened, but he hurried back to Cuzco as soon as he heard the good news. He was excited to hear that his brother had finally been defeated. He was ready to become the next emperor of the Inca Empire.

Huáscar, who was defeated
Source: https://commons.wikimedia.org/wiki/File:Waskhar_
portrait.jpg#/media/File:Waskhar_portrait.jpg

Atahualpa didn't get to enjoy his victory, though. Can you imagine how frustrating that would be? Atahualpa had just fought a war to become the emperor, and he didn't even get to enjoy it. Have you ever worked hard for something and then had it taken away from you before you got to enjoy it? It's really upsetting when that happens! For Atahualpa, it was even worse. He didn't just lose the throne. He lost the whole empire.

In November 1532, Atahualpa was celebrating his victory when the **Spanish conquistadors** finally arrived. Atahualpa agreed to meet the Spaniards because he thought they were going to pay him tribute as the new emperor. Instead, they took him prisoner and demanded that he swear loyalty to them! To make it worse, the tribes didn't come to rescue him because he had terrorized them during the civil war. In a few short years, the Inca Empire would end.

Emperor Atahualpa, the victorious brother
Source: https://commons.wikimedia.org/wiki/File:Ataw_Wallpa_portrait.jpg#/media/File:Ataw_Wallpa_portrait.jpg

There were a variety of problems that caused the downfall of the Inca Empire. The Incas could not find enough workers because of all the diseases that were sweeping through Central and South America. The pandemic killed at least half of the people, which made it hard for the

Incas to get anything done. They were also dealing with rebellions from smaller tribes as they continued to expand. The final problem was the civil war. It weakened the empire even more. All three of these problems worked together to bring about the fall of the Incas. When the Spanish conquistadors arrived, they took advantage of the bad situation the Incas were dealing with and finished the downfall of the mighty Inca Empire.

Chapter 6 Challenge: Matching

Can you match the word or phrase with the description that goes with it?

1. Emperor Atahualpa

    a. Some of the diseases that killed 50 to 90 percent of the people living in Central and South America.

2. Smallpox and influenza

    b. The emperor whose death caused the Inca Civil War.

3. Spanish conquistadors

    c. The brother who lost the Inca Civil War.

4. Huáscar

    d. The new capital the Incas established in modern-day Ecuador.

5. Quito

    e. The brother who won the Inca Civil War.

6. Emperor Huayna Capac

    f. The people who finally defeated the Inca Empire.

Chapter 7: The Spanish Conquest

Although the Inca Empire was strong at the height of its power, the Spanish conquest of the Inca civilization was very quick. This was because the Spanish conquistadors arrived during a rough time for the Incas. With so many problems going on at once, the Incas weren't able to properly fight the Spanish conquistadors until it was too late.

The **Spanish conquistadors** were explorers from Spain. They came to Central and South America looking for gold and other valuable items. They wanted to become rich and powerful. They had heard that some of the civilizations in Central and South America had a lot of gold and silver. They didn't know much else about any of the people who lived there. The Spanish conquistadors didn't know that the civilizations in

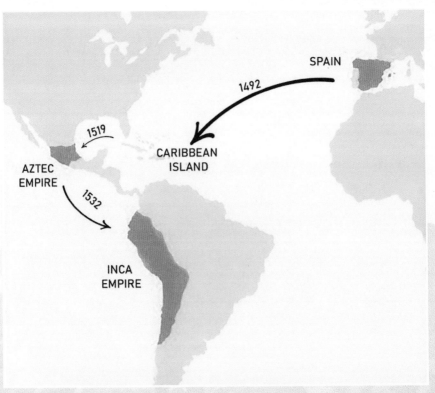

Map of the Aztec and Inca empires at the time of the Spanish conquest

Central and South America had rich and interesting cultures. Some of them thought they were bringing civilization to the people who lived there without realizing they were destroying civilizations that were simply different from their own.

The Spanish conquistador who led the conquest of the Inca Empire was **Francisco Pizarro**. He was born around 1475 in a small town in Spain. He grew up poor and often dreamed of leaving behind his small town and his job as a pig herder. When he heard that there was gold and adventure in the **New World**, he jumped at the chance to leave Spain and find a better future. The Spanish called Central and South America the "New World" because it was brand-new to them. Would you have been able to leave everything you knew and go to a new world? It was very brave of Francisco Pizarro to do that!

Francisco Pizarro first arrived in the New World around 1502. He helped with other Spanish conquests before he got permission from the king of Spain to lead his own conquest in 1532. When Francisco Pizarro arrived in the Inca Empire, he found a land that was full of gold. He also saw that there were a lot of problems going on. He decided to take advantage of those problems and overthrow the Incas to conquer their land and riches.

When Francisco Pizarro arrived in the Inca Empire, the Inca Civil War was finishing. Atahualpa had defeated his half-brother and was preparing to take the throne as the next Inca emperor. On November 16th, 1532, Francisco Pizarro offered to meet Atahualpa at **Cajamarca**, a city in northern Peru, for a celebratory feast. This was a lie. Francisco Pizarro did not want to congratulate Atahualpa for becoming the next emperor of the Incas. He wanted to conquer the Incas for the king of Spain and become their new governor.

Francisco didn't explain this to the Incas, though. Instead, he hid his soldiers and had **Friar Vicente de Valverde** approach Atahualpa. He and Francisco told Atahualpa that he should swear loyalty to **King Charles I**, the king of Spain and give his kingdom to the king. They also told Atahualpa that he needed to convert to Christianity because it was the only true religion. The friar handed him a Bible and told him that all the answers to life's biggest questions were in that book.

Francisco Pizarro meets with the Inca emperor Atahualpa, 1532
Source: https://commons.wikimedia.org/wiki/File:Atawallpa_
Pizarro_tinkuy.jpg#/media/File:Atawallpa_Pizarro_tinkuy.jpg

Can you imagine how confusing that must have been for Atahualpa? He had just become emperor and had come for a party. Now, these strangers wanted him to give up his kingdom and his religious views just because they said so. He didn't even understand what the Bible was or how it could tell him the answers to life's questions. Atahualpa had never seen a book before and did not know how to read. He certainly didn't know how to read Spanish! When the Bible did not begin to speak to him, he threw it on the ground in disgust.

Francisco Pizarro did not understand how he had confused Atahualpa. Instead, he thought that Atahualpa was disrespecting Christianity by throwing the Bible on the ground. Francisco Pizarro took that as an opportunity to open fire. This started the **Battle of Cajamarca**, but it was really more of a **massacre**. The Incas had not brought any weapons with them because they were expecting to come to a party. You don't bring weapons to a party! Within an hour, the Spanish had killed all of the Incas in the room except for Atahualpa. He was captured, and Francisco Pizarro held him for ransom while the Spanish captured the rest of the city.

A drawing of the Battle of Cajamarca
Source: https://commons.wikimedia.org/wiki/File:Inca-Spanish_
confrontation.JPG#/media/File:Inca-Spanish_confrontation.JPG

Atahualpa realized that he was in a lot of trouble. Things were not going well for him, so he tried to save himself by offering Francisco Pizarro a lot of money. In fact, he offered him a room full of gold and silver. That would have been enough money for Francisco Pizarro to live comfortably for the rest of his life! Francisco took the money, but he didn't let Atahualpa go. Instead, he ordered Atahualpa to be executed on July 26th, 1533.

At first, they were going to burn him at the stake because he had not converted to Christianity. Atahualpa didn't want to die like that. Friar Vicente de Valverde said that if he converted to Christianity, they wouldn't burn him at the stake. The Spanish said they would give him a more merciful death and postpone his execution. Atahualpa thought that sounded better, and he converted. The Spanish killed him on August 29th, 1533.

THE EXECUTION OF THE INCA.

Execution of Atahualpa on July 26th, 1533
Source: https://commons.wikimedia.org/wiki/File:The_
execution_of_Inca.jpg#/media/File:The_execution_of_Inca.jpg

After killing the Inca emperor, Francisco Pizarro wanted to conquer Cuzco. The Spanish set up Tupac Huallpa as the new Inca emperor, but he died after only a few months. The Spanish then chose **Manco Inca** as the new emperor to help them capture Cuzco. They marched into the city and then began to loot it. Manco Inca did not like what the Spanish were doing to his people. He rebelled against them in 1536, but there was not much he could do to stop their conquest. He wasn't able to rescue Cuzco, and he had to retreat to the mountains. Some Inca resistance continued in the mountains for a few years, but even that was eventually put down by the Spanish conquistadors.

Francisco Pizarro set out for the Inca Empire to conquer it, and he certainly did. The diseases that he accidentally brought with him killed thousands of Incas. The people who survived the diseases were often killed by the Spanish. The population of the Inca Empire declined rapidly during the Spanish conquest. The Spanish didn't just kill many of the Incas. They also destroyed their cities and their culture. They built new cities on the ruins of the old ones, and they replaced the Inca culture with their Spanish culture. Although a few Incas managed to survive these hard times, much of the Inca culture was lost forever to the Spanish conquest of the New World.

Chapter 7 Challenge: Fill in the Blank

Can you fill in the blank in the sentences below with the correct vocabulary word?

> New World   Friar Vicente de Valverde   Atahualpa   Manco Inca
>
> Battle of Cajamarca   gold and silver   Francisco Pizzaro   diseases

1. _____ arrived in the Inca Empire in 1532.

2. The first battle of the Spanish conquest of the Incas was the _____.

3. Atahualpa paid the Spanish a room full of _____ after getting captured.

4. Francisco Pizarro captured _____ on November 16th, 1532, by pretending to throw a celebratory feast in his honor.

5. _____ converted Atahualpa to Christianity before his execution.

6. The Spanish made _____ the new emperor to help them get into Cuzco.

7. The Inca population declined quickly because of the _____ the Spanish brought with them.

8. The Spanish called Central and South America the _____.

Chapter 8: Famous Inca Rulers

Although the Incas had proven themselves to be fierce and strong, the Inca Empire only lasted for about 200 years. When you look at all of history, 200 years isn't actually a lot of time!

During their 200 years, the Incas had 18 rulers, and we'll be covering the most important ones in this chapter. The 18 Inca rulers can be split up into three groups. The first eight rulers were kings before the Incas established their empire. This time is called **the pre-imperial era**. The next six rulers were emperors. The last four rulers did not rule from Cuzco. Instead, they led the Inca rebellion against the Spanish conquistadors from a city in the mountains called **Vilcabamba**. The Inca rulers all helped create one of the greatest empires in the Americas.

Manco Cápac (1200-1230 CE)

Manco Cápac was the first king of the Incas. There are myths that he was the son of **Inti**, the sun god, but historians think that Manco Cápac

Manco Cápac

was a normal person just like us. He ruled the Incas from about 1200 to 1230 CE. He was married to Mama Ocllo, who also played a part in the myth of how the Incas began their civilization. Historians know that Manco Cápac came up with the first laws that the Incas followed. He also built the first Temple of the Sun. Manco Cápac emphasized how important it was to worship Inti properly, and the Incas would follow this example while they ruled the western coast of South America.

Sinchi Roca (1230-1260 CE)

Sinchi Roca was the son of Manco Cápac. He ruled the Incas from 1230 to 1260 CE. Historians think that Sinchi Roca was the first Inca king to wear royal garments and jewelry. One of those items was the imperial crown, which the Incas called the **Mascaipacha**. Sinchi Roca also fought wars with the tribes around Cuzco to protect the city. He also wanted to expand the empire. Just like his father, Sinchi Roca took his religion seriously. He ordered more construction on the Temple of the Sun to make it bigger and more impressive.

Sinchi Roca
Source: https://commons.wikimedia.org/wiki/File:SAHUARAURA_p049_-_SINCHI_ROCCA.jpg#/media/Archivo:SAHUARAURA_p049_-_SINCHI_ROCCA.jpg

Mayta Cápac (1290-1320 CE)

Mayta Cápac was the fourth king, and he is best remembered for all the battles he fought. He had to work really hard to keep Cuzco safe from tribes who wanted to take it. He also had to work hard to continue to get more land for the Incas. Mayta Cápac started to move the Incas into the highlands around Cuzco.

Cápac Yupanqui (1320-1350 CE)

Cápac Yupanqui was the fifth king, and he is best remembered for being the first Inca ruler to conquer any land outside of Cuzco Valley! He wasn't technically the rightful ruler of the Incas. But he was so powerful that most people accepted him instead of **Inca Tarco Huaman**, who was Mayta Cápac's son.

Cápac Yupanqui was very good at making military alliances. He made an alliance with the **Ayarmaca** tribe to fight against the **Chanca** people. The Chancas were numerous and powerful. The Incas wanted to get rid of them so that they could become the most powerful civilization. Sadly, Cápac Yupanqui died before he was able to fight the Chancas, so other Incas had to continue the fight for him.

Pachacuti (1438-1471 CE)

Pachacuti was the ninth ruler and the first emperor of the Incas. He was the ruler who first started the Inca Empire! Pachacuti first came into power while the Incas were fighting the Chancas. He kicked them out of Cuzco and declared himself the next king because his father had fled the city instead of staying to protect the people. Pachacuti then rebuilt Cuzco to be even better than before. Some historians think that Pachacuti shaped Cuzco to look like a jaguar or a puma. Pachacuti also built Machu Picchu. He greatly expanded the Inca Empire and refined the laws. He was one of the most important and best-remembered of all the Inca rulers.

Pachacuti

Source: https://commons.wikimedia.org/wiki/File:
PachacutecIXinca.jpg#/media/File:PachacutecIXinca.jpg

Huáscar (1527-1532 CE)

Huáscar was the fifth emperor of the Inca Empire. He spent most of his reign in a fierce civil war with his half-brother Atahualpa. Huáscar was afraid that someone was going to overthrow him. After his father **Huayna Capac** died of smallpox, Huáscar had several of his brothers killed because he thought they were plotting to overthrow him. Paranoia can be dangerous! Huáscar lost the civil war with his half-brother Atahualpa, and Atahualpa had him killed.

Atahualpa (1532-1533 CE)

Atahualpa was the last true Inca emperor. His reign was really short! Just as he was defeating his half-brother Huáscar, the **Spanish conquistadors** arrived. They tricked Atahualpa into coming to a meeting with them, and then they captured him. Atahualpa didn't even get to claim his throne in Cuzco. He paid the Spanish a lot of gold and silver as a ransom to let him go. The Spanish decided to take his money and then kill him. His death officially ended the Inca Empire, and **Spanish colonization** began to spread throughout the land.

Manco Inca II (1533-1544 CE)

Manco Inca II was made king by the Spanish. That might seem a little strange. Why would the Spanish give the Incas another king if they wanted to conquer the Incas? The Spanish wanted to rule from the shadows. They thought it would be easier to conquer the people if the Incas thought there was still a Sapa Inca (the title of their ruler) in

Manco Inca II
Source: https://commons.wikimedia.org/wiki/File:SAHUARAURA_
p108_MANCO_INCA.jpg#/media/Archivo:SAHUARAURA_p108_MANCO_INCA.jpg

charge. It might have worked, except Manco Inca II saw the horrible things the Spanish were doing to his people. He rebelled. He left Cuzco and made **Vilcabamba** his main city in 1537. From there, he fought against the Spanish conquest until his death in 1544.

Túpac Amaru (1571-1572 CE)

Túpac Amaru was the last Inca ruler. He fought hard against the Spanish, but by this point, there were too many Spanish conquistadors in the area. He was eventually captured when he fled from Vilcabamba. The Spanish had him put to death in 1572 in the Plaza de Armas in Cuzco. After Túpac Amaru died, there were no more kings of the Incas. Túpac Amaru was the last of a long line of strong, wise, and fierce rulers.

Túpac Amaru

Source: https://commons.wikimedia.org/wiki/File:Tupaq_
Amaru_I_hapisqa.gif#/media/File:Tupaq_Amaru_I_hapisqa.gif

Chapter 8 Challenge: Timeline Activity

Can you put the names of the Incas rulers in the correct order? Draw a line on your paper to help you get each one in the right spot in time.

! Túpac Amaru

! Atahualpa

! Pachacuti

! Mayta Cápac

! Manco Cápac

! Sinchi Roca

! Cápac Yupanqui

! Huáscar

! Manco Inca II

Chapter 9: Inca Myths and Gods

Mythology was important to the Incas. They had several different gods and goddesses that they worshiped in temples across the Inca Empire. Although they didn't leave us any written notes about their gods, religion was clearly important to the Incas. Their temples were carefully built and were beautifully decorated. People don't take that kind of time to make something like that unless it is very important to them.

We have a few myths from the Incas, but most of these myths deal with the creation of the world and the start of the Inca people. They likely had other myths, but those stories never got written down. Sadly, this means they've been forgotten. The myths we do have were written down by the Spanish conquistadors when they conquered the Incas. Although many of the conquistadors were only focused on power and money, a few of them thought the Incas were interesting and wrote down some things about them.

The Creation Myth

The **Inca creation myth** starts in total darkness. **Viracocha** is the creator god in Inca mythology, and the first world he created was pitch dark and full of **giants**. Would you want to live in a world like that? Viracocha eventually got angry with the giants. They were always disobeying him. So, he destroyed the giants and the dark world.

There are different versions of the story at this point. Some stories say that Viracocha wiped out all the giants with a huge flood, but other stories say that he turned the giants into stone.

Either way, Viracocha got rid of the giants. Then he tried again. He made a second world and filled this world with smaller creatures that were made out of clay. These smaller creatures were people. Viracocha made them look like him. He also gave them light, clothes, language, and food. Viracocha gave the humans everything they needed to be happy and healthy. Then he scattered the humans across the face of the earth.

The Origin of the Incas

The Incas have a different myth of **the creation of the Inca Empire.** As the story goes, when the people were first created, they didn't know anything about how to live like people. They ran around without clothes on, slept on the ground without any houses, and acted like wild animals. Have you ever learned something for the first time? It's hard at first because you don't know what you're doing. No one had ever taught the first people how to be people, so they weren't very good at it.

The gods were sad when they watched the humans act like wild animals. They took pity on them. **Inti** decided to send one of his sons down to

OCCLLO HVACO ECOYA.

A painting of Mama Ocllo
Source: https://en.wikipedia.org/wiki/Mama_Ocllo#/media/File:
Mama_Ocllo,_Peru,_circa_1840,_San_Antonio_Museum_of_Art.jpg

Earth to help the people learn how to be good humans. He sent **Manco Cápac** and his wife **Mama Ocllo**. When they arrived on Earth, they appeared to the Inca tribe and immediately began teaching them how to weave clothes and farm food. They also taught the people how to make and use weapons so they could defend themselves and make their empire grow.

They also told the people how important it was to worship Inti properly. Inti wasn't upset because the people didn't know better, but they now had to make sure to worship the sun god correctly. All of the Incas left their small village and followed Manco Cápac in search of the right place to worship Inti. They were looking for a place where a golden stake could be driven into the ground with only one hit. After a lot of looking, they finally found the spot. They built the city of **Cuzco** there to be the new capital of the Inca people.

The Great Flood

Almost every civilization has a flood story. The Inca's **flood story** goes like this. Before Manco Cápac came to teach the Incas how to be strong and powerful, everyone in the world was bad. They all did bad things, and this upset the gods. The gods planned to flood the whole world and start over again. There were only two young shepherds who were good. They were brothers, and they tended **llamas** all day long in the mountains.

One day, they noticed that their llamas looked sad. When the boys asked about it, the llamas told them about the coming flood. The brothers quickly got their family and their herds of animals into high caves in the mountains. When the rains fell and drowned the whole world, the people in the caves survived. Once the rain stopped, Inti dried up all the extra water, the people came out of their caves and repopulated the world.

Meeting the Inca Gods

There are several important gods and goddesses in Inca mythology. Each of these **deities** had a different part to play in the Inca **pantheon** or ruling group of gods. However, they were all important to the Incas.

Viracocha was the creator god. He's the one who was responsible for making everything. That includes the other gods, Earth, the heavens, and the people. Although he wasn't really active in the lives of the Incas, they were still respectful of Viracocha. The Incas had a myth in which some people weren't grateful for all Viracocha had made. When he heard them complain, he turned them into stone! Turning into stone doesn't sound like fun, so the Incas were careful to be respectful of the creator god.

Viracocha

Inti was probably the most important god in the daily lives of the Incas. He was the sun god, and the Incas believed that their kings were direct descendants of him. They had temples for Inti in important places throughout the Inca Empire. The walls and floors of the temples were covered in gold. The Inca believed that gold was special to Inti because it was the sun's sweat. The most famous Temple of the Sun is **Coricancha** in Cuzco.

An Inca king worshiping Inti

Mama Quilla was the moon goddess. She was both Inti's sister and his wife. We might think that's a little weird, but the Incas did not think it was weird for royal siblings to marry each other. As the moon goddess, Mama Quilla was in charge of the calendar, marriage, and protecting women. The Incas kept their calendar by the phases of the moon, so

Mama Quilla was an important part of Inca culture. Her temple was covered in silver because the Incas thought that silver was the moon's tears.

There were several other Inca gods. **Coniraya** was the male moon god who helped with creating life. **Mama Cocha** was the goddess of the sea. **Pachamama** was the goddess of the earth. She was in charge of giving the Incas a good harvest. **Illapu** was the god of weather. He gave rain to the Incas for crops.

The Incas took their religion very seriously because they believed their gods helped them to survive. The myths we have from the Incas show them explaining how they came to exist and how their gods helped them become powerful conquerors of the Pacific coast of South America.

Chapter 9 Challenge: Creative Activity

Inca mythology is full of gods helping out people who need it. Although the gods can be a little harsh when people aren't grateful, they also helped the Incas. The Incas used their mythology to show they were better than the tribes they were conquering.

Let's write our own Inca myth! Take one of the historical events you have learned about in this book and write it as a new Inca myth. Pick your favorite Inca ruler, and write about how the gods helped (or didn't help) him to defend Cuzco or expand the Inca Empire. You can use one or two different gods in your new myth, and make sure you include three to five facts about the historical event in your myth. Remember, the Incas mixed their history with their mythology, so some of their myths have parts that probably happened. Then have fun writing about how one (or more) of the Inca gods helped the Incas solve their problems!

Chapter 10: Society and Government

The Incas didn't just spend their lives conquering other tribes. They actually built a complex society for themselves that had a strong government, distinct social classes, and even rules for education and marriage. That's really advanced! A lot of societies take a long time to develop everything the Incas had.

The Incas had strict social classes. In modern times, we often aren't bound by the social class we are born into. We can better ourselves by working hard and making good choices. The Incas did not have that option. They couldn't change their social class. They couldn't even change their jobs if they wanted to! As soon as you were old enough to work, you were assigned a job, and that was all you did for the rest of your life.

There were three social classes in the Inca Empire. The first social class was the **noble class**. They were also called the **Inca class**. The nobles were the people whose ancestors had first established Cuzco. Their job was to run the government, and they held the most powerful positions. They made most of the big decisions and were in charge of the cities and regions of the empire. The king was the most important person in the noble class.

The second social class was the **public administrator class**. These people were in charge of the lower-level jobs in the government. They would do things like collect taxes, design buildings, and keep records like a secretary does today. These people were important because they kept the whole empire going. However, the Incas didn't think they were as important as the nobility.

The third social class was the **commoner class**. These were the craftsmen and the farmers. Craftsmen made all sorts of things, like pottery and gold items. Most people in the Inca Empire were farmers. Even though the farmers were thought of as being at the lowest level in society, they were very important. Without the hard work of the farmers, the Inca Empire would not have survived very long. The farmers sent two-thirds of their harvest to the government, which is how everyone who wasn't a farmer was able to eat.

You might have noticed that we haven't mentioned slaves. Even though the Incas fought in a lot of wars, they didn't take people as slaves. In fact, they didn't have any slaves at all! Instead, everyone in the empire was part of an **ayllu**. An ayllu is a group of families who all work together like one big extended family. The ayllu was the basic unit for the whole empire.

The ayllu was a big part of everyone's lives, but the Inca Empire's government also played a big part. The Inca Empire was very large, so

The Sapa Inca surrounded by noble representatives
Source: https://commons.wikimedia.org/wiki/File:Consejo_Inca.jpg#/media/File:Consejo_Inca.jpg

the government had to be organized and strong. The Inca Empire's government was a **monarchy**. The king, who was also called the **Sapa Inca**, was in charge of everything. Of course, the Sapa Inca did not make every decision in the whole government. Can you imagine how overwhelming that would be? Instead, the king had **royal advisors** who helped him make the big decisions.

The empire was split up into four sections. This would be like states or provinces of modern-day countries. Each section was called a **suyu**, and each suyu had a governor, who was called an **apu**. The apu made decisions for his personal suyu, much like how a governor makes decisions for their state. They reported to the king, but the king didn't have to make every decision for them. There were also other officials. Some of these officials were priests, inspectors, military generals, and tax collectors.

Taxes were a big deal for the Incas. Their empire was so large that not having taxes would have ruined them. There were two ways that people had to pay taxes. The first tax was a **crops tax**. Each ayllu gave one-third of their crops to the government and one-third to the temples. They were allowed to keep the final third to eat. The second tax was a labor tax called a **mit'a**. For part of the year, all men ages 16 through 60 had to work on a government project. There were lots of different projects. After all, there were always roads to build, gold to mine, and battles to fight.

There were laws in the Inca Empire about taxes and other things, like murder and stealing. There wasn't a lot of crime because the punishments were so harsh. If someone heard you curse the gods, you could be executed! The punishments were harsh to keep people from breaking the laws, and it usually worked.

Most people in the Inca Empire did not spend their lives worrying about the government punishing them. Most of them were busy just living their lives. The commoners lived in small houses made from **adobe bricks**. Their houses didn't have windows or solid doors. Their doorways were usually covered with a piece of leather or woven cloth. They slept on mats on the floor. When they weren't sleeping, they were supposed to be working. Even children worked! As soon as children were old enough to do something, they were working. Inca children didn't have a lot of time to play.

It was a hard life for most of the Incas, but they usually had plenty to eat. The Incas ate corn, beans, and squash. Depending on where they lived, some people also ate tomatoes, fish, duck, and peppers. The farmers worked hard to grow enough food for the whole empire. The government was responsible for distributing it to everyone. That way, the people who didn't farm or who couldn't farm because of an injury or old age still had plenty to eat.

The clothing and hairstyles of the Incas were used to show one's place in society. Everyone wore the same type of clothes. Men wore sleeveless tunics, and women wore long dresses. The clothing of the nobles was much nicer, and the commoners' clothing was made of coarse wool. Hairstyles were the main way that the Incas separated themselves into classes. Each ayllu had its own special hairstyle, and you wore your hair like your ayllu to show who your family was. The Incas were concerned about social classes, so your hairstyle was a lot more than something you decided on every morning before going to school. Speaking of school, the Inca schools were very different from our schools. Only upper-class boys went to school, and they had three to four years of education.

Sketches of Inca nobles in full costumes

The Incas' lives were shaped by their social classes and government.
Everything was organized and carefully planned out. It seems that the
Incas were satisfied. They helped each other and loved their families.
Beneath their tough warrior attitudes, the Incas built a society that
tried to take care of everyone.

Chapter 10 Challenge: Dig Deeper

The Inca society was rich and complex. This chapter only scratches the surface! Pick a topic from this chapter you want to know more about, and do some research. Here are a few examples to get you started:

! What other kinds of government positions reported to the Sapa Inca?

! What are some examples of Inca hairstyles? Can you make your hair look like that? Make sure to ask for help at home before doing any big makeovers.

! What kinds of houses did the nobles live in?

There are also other topics you can explore! If none of the topics from this chapter interest you, try researching one of these topics instead!

! Childcare in the Inca Empire

! Marriage traditions

! How children were educated

! All the jobs that government inspectors did

! Specialized jobs, such as "chosen women" and herders

If you want to learn more about tons of other exciting
historical periods, check out our other books!

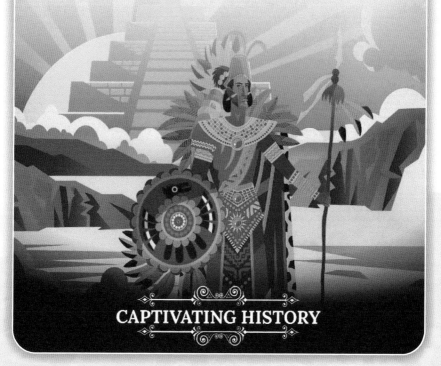

AZTEC HISTORY
FOR KIDS

A CAPTIVATING GUIDE TO THE AZTEC EMPIRE AND CIVILIZATION, FROM THE AZTECS SETTLING IN THE VALLEY OF MEXICO TO THE SPANISH CONQUEST

CAPTIVATING HISTORY

Bibliography

"Biography: Francisco Pizarro." *Ducksters*. Accessed December 2021
https://www.ducksters.com/biography/explorers/francisco_pizarro.php

Britannica, T. Editors of Encyclopedia. "Chimú." *Encyclopedia Britannica*.
August 30, 2021. https://www.britannica.com/topic/Chimu

Britannica, T. Editors of Encyclopedia. "Huari." *Encyclopedia Britannica*.
March 7, 2016. https://www.britannica.com/place/Huari

Britannica, T. Editors of Encyclopedia. "Inca." *Encyclopedia Britannica*.
September 21, 2021. https://www.britannica.com/topic/Inca

Britannica, T. Editors of Encyclopedia. "Machu Picchu." *Encyclopedia
Britannica*, October 6, 2021. https://www.britannica.com/place/Machu-
Picchu

Britannica, T. Editors of Encyclopedia. "Tiwanaku." *Encyclopedia Britannica*.
January 29, 2019. https://www.britannica.com/place/Tiwanaku

Cartwright, Mark. "Coricancha." *Word History Encyclopedia*. UNESCO
Archives. March 9, 2014. https://www.worldhistory.org/Coricancha

Cartwright, Mark. "Cusco." *Word History Encyclopedia*. UNESCO Archives.
January 30, 2015. https://www.worldhistory.org/Cuzco

Cartwright, Mark. "Inca Civilization." *Word History Encyclopedia*. UNESCO
Archives. September 15, 2014.
https://www.worldhistory.org/Inca_Civilization

Cartwright, Mark. "Pachacuti Inca Yupanqui." *Word History Encyclopedia*.
UNESCO Archives. July 18, 2016.
https://www.worldhistory.org/Pachacuti_Inca_Yupanqui

Editors, History.com. "Inca." *History*. March 11, 2015.
https://www.history.com/topics/south-america/inca

Editors, History.com. "Machu Picchu." *History*. June 13, 2011.
https://www.history.com/topics/south-america/inca

Editors, History.com. "Francisco Pizarro traps Incan emperor Atahualpa."
History. November 10, 2021. https://www.history.com/this-day-in-
history/pizarro-traps-incan-emperor-atahualpa

"Inca Civilization Timeline." *Ancient History Encyclopedia*. Accessed

December 2021. https://www.ancient.eu/timeline/Inca_Civilization

"Inca Daily Life." *History's Histories*. Accessed December 2021. http://www.historyshistories.com/inca-daily-life.html

"Inca Empire: Cuzco City." *Ducksters*. Accessed December 2021. https://www.ducksters.com/history/inca/cuzco.php

"Inca Empire: Daily Life." *Ducksters*. Accessed December 2021. https://www.ducksters.com/history/inca/daily_life.php

"Inca Empire: Government." *Ducksters*. Accessed December 2021. https://www.ducksters.com/history/inca/government.php

"Inca Empire: Tribes of Early Peru." *Ducksters*. Accessed November 2021. https://www.ducksters.com/history/inca/tribes_of_early_peru.php

"Inca Empire: Mythology and Religion." *Ducksters*. Accessed December 2021. https://www.ducksters.com/history/inca/mythology_and_religion.php

"Inca Empire: Society." *Ducksters*. Accessed December 2021. https://www.ducksters.com/history/inca/society.php

"Inca Mythology." *Myths and Legends*. Myth Encyclopedia. Accessed December 2021. http://www.mythencyclopedia.com/Ho-Iv/Inca-Mythology.html

Jarus, Owen. "The Inca Empire." *Live Science*. Future US Inc. November 5, 2018. https://www.livescience.com/41346-the-incas-history-of-andean-empire.html

"Machu Picchu." *Wikipedia, the Free Encyclopedia*. Accessed December 2021. https://en.wikipedia.org/wiki/Machu_Picchu#Inti_Mach'ay_and_the_Royal_Feast_of_the_Sun

Minister, Christopher. "Huáscar and Atahualpa Inca Civil War." *ThoughtCo*. February 18, 2019. https://www.thoughtco.com/huascar-and-atahualpa-inca-civil-war-2136539

"Origin Myths of the Inca Empire." *Tailormade Experiences by Inca Rail*. 2018. https://blogs.incarail.com/origin-legends-of-the-inca-empire

"Pre-Inca Civilizations." *Discover Peru*. Accessed November 2021. http://www.discover-peru.org/pre-inca-civilizations

"Pre-Inca Civilizations in Peru." *Kuoda Personalized Travel*. 2020. https://www.kuodatravel.com/how-to-travel-peru/ancient-peru/pre-incan-civilizations

"Sacsayhuaman: Everything You Need to Know about the Inca Fortress." *Ticket Machu Picchu*. Accessed December 2021. https://www.ticketmachupicchu.com/fortress-sacsayhuaman

"Short History of the Incas." *Chimu Blog*. Chimu Adventures. November 22, 2016. https://www.chimuadventures.com/blog/2016/11/incas-short-history

"The 14 Incas of Tahuantinsuyo." *Tailormade Experiences by Inca Rail.* 2018. https://blogs.incarail.com/14-incas-of-tahuantinsuyo

"The Caral Civilization." *World Civilization*. Boundless World History. Accessed November 2021. https://courses.lumenlearning.com/suny-hccc-worldcivilization/chapter/the-caral-civilization

"The Conquest of the Inca Empire." *The Spanish War History*. 2012. https://www.spanishwars.net/16th-century-conquest-inca-empire.html

"The Fall of the Inca Empire." *Discover Peru*. Accessed December 2021. http://www.discover-peru.org/the-fall-of-the-inca-empire

"Who Were the Inca Rulers?" *Ticket Machu Picchu*. Accessed December 2021. https://www.ticketmachupicchu.com/inca-emperors/#inca-rulers.

Suggested Reading List

Sandra Newman. *The Inca Empire (A True Book: Ancient Civilizations)*. 2010.

Colin Hynson. *You Wouldn't Want to Be an Inca Mummy!* 2007.

Jane Bingham. *Inca Empire (Time Travel Guide)*. 2007.

Printed in Great Britain
by Amazon

80273597R00047